Ella Bella Boon

Written by Peter Bently

Illustrated by Sophia Touliatou

OXFORD
UNIVERSITY PRESS

OXFORD
UNIVERSITY PRESS

Great Clarendon Street, Oxford, OX2 6DP, United Kingdom

Oxford University Press is a department of the University of Oxford. It furthers the University's objective of excellence in research, scholarship, and education by publishing worldwide. Oxford is a registered trade mark of Oxford University Press in the UK and in certain other countries

Text © Peter Bently 2017
Illustrations © Sophia Touliatou 2017
Inside cover notes written by Karra McFarlane

The moral rights of the author have been asserted

First published 2017

All rights reserved. No part of this publication may be reproduced, stored in a retrieval system, or transmitted, in any form or by any means, without the prior permission in writing of Oxford University Press, or as expressly permitted by law, by licence or under terms agreed with the appropriate reprographics rights organization. Enquiries concerning reproduction outside the scope of the above should be sent to the Rights Department, Oxford University Press, at the address above.

You must not circulate this work in any other form and you must impose this same condition on any acquirer

British Library Cataloguing in Publication Data
Data available

ISBN: 978-0-19-841501-5

15

Paper used in the production of this book is a natural, recyclable product made from wood grown in sustainable forests. The manufacturing process conforms to the environmental regulations of the country of origin.

Printed in China by Shanghai Offset Printing Products Ltd

Acknowledgements
Series Editor: Nikki Gamble

The manufacturer's authorised representative in the EU for product safety is Oxford University Press España S.A. of El Parque Empresarial San Fernando de Henares, Avenida de Castilla, 2 – 28830 Madrid (www.oup.cs/cn or product.safety@oup.com). OUP España S.A. also acts as importer into Spain of products made by the manufacturer.

This is Ella Bella Boon.
She had a farm on Mix-up Moon.

At night she got up from her bed and put her boot upon her head.

She put her hats upon her feet,
then went to get an egg to eat.

She went to her cow with sixteen legs.
The cow was red and laid big eggs.

She took an egg but in the dark she fell on the cow and it started to bark!

"Woof!" went the cow, then the sheep went "Quack!"

Ella went "Eek!" and the egg went **crack!**

But Ella was not sad for long.
She drank her chips and sang a song.